PAPERBACK PLUS Teacher's Resource — W9-AUF-279

At a Glance: In the Cow's Backyard   2

Choices for Reading and Assessment   3

Setting the Stage   4
   Book Summary

   Introducing the Theme

   Building Background

   Introducing the Book

   Choices for Reading

Exploring the Book   6
   Each section includes

   Summary

   Developing Vocabulary

   Reading Strategies

   Discussion Questions

   Activities

PAPERBACK PLUS Activities   12

Activity Masters
   Activity Master 1: All Together *(Language Patterns)*   13

   Activity Master 2: Which Came Next? *(Sequence)*   14

   Activity Master 3: Share-the-Pool Party *(Problem Solving)*   15

Assessment   16

Bibliography

In the Cow's Backyard

In this twist on the old adage that "there's always room for one more," an ant relaxes in a hammock under the cow's shade tree. Soon, at the ant's invitation, a frog, a chick, a hen, a duck, a cat, a dog, and a lamb are all crowding in and unwittingly testing the hammock's strength. Suspense builds when a mother elephant shows up. Is there room for her as well? Will the hammock break? The elephant's surprising solution shows that good friends can always find a way to share.

In the Cow's Backyard

- Children will enjoy sharing the author and illustrator information.

- The story's predictable sentence patterns and cumulative text invite children to read independently or chorally.

- Colorful illustrations add humor to the story and convey the animals' dilemma.

- There's always room for one more good friend—but how many is too many? This story illustrates that "good-will" can help lead to a satisfying solution.

PAPERBACK PLUS

So Many Kinds of Animals
(pages 24–25)

- This poem by Mary Ann Hoberman, with art by Malcah Zeldis, celebrates the variety in the animal kingdom.

It's So-o-o HOT!
(pages 26–27)

- A photo essay from *Chickadee* magazine shows how different desert animals deal with hot weather. The simple multiple-choice questions encourage children to look closely at the photos and draw conclusions.

Sardines
(page 28)

- Children will get a chance to re-create the problem in the story as they play this variation on the classic game of hide–and–seek.

Reading Options

Depending on children's needs and interests, choose one of the following options for the whole book, or alternate options to read the book in segments. For all options, use the Discussion Questions on page 5, or children's own questions about the book, to establish a purpose for reading.

Reading Aloud

Choose one of these options for reading aloud:

Option 1: Read the entire book aloud. Model reading strategies by stopping to share your thoughts about the text.

Option 2: Read the whole book aloud without stopping. Then reread it using the Exploring the Book sections, starting on page 6.

Option 3: Read the book aloud using option 1 or 2, and have children follow along in their own books.

Guided Reading

Have children read the book in segments, as a class or in groups. After each segment, use the Discussion Questions or children's own questions to talk about what they have read.

Cooperative Reading

Have children read the whole book in pairs or in small groups, helping each other with the text.

Independent Reading

Assign the book, and have children read it independently.

Reading Strategies

One or more of the following strategies are recommended for each segment of the book: Predict/Infer, Self-Question, Monitor, Evaluate, Summarize. Depending on children's needs and the focus of your lessons, you may choose to follow these recommendations, to use a different strategy, or to use all the strategies.

Informal Assessment

The Paperback Plus Teacher's Resource provides opportunities for both student self-assessment and informal assessment by the teacher. Ongoing self-assessment offers children a chance to reflect on and evaluate their thinking about what they have read. Student discussions give you many opportunities to observe and assess children's progress. The Informal Assessment Checklist on page 16 can be used during student/teacher conferences.

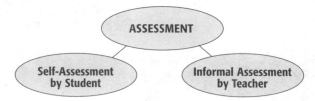

Activities

You can use the responding and cross-curricular activities to assess children's ability to understand and apply what they have read. Children can work independently or in small groups to complete the activities. You may wish to assign particular activities or to copy and distribute these pages for children to choose from.

Activity Masters

You can use these blackline masters as minilessons or as tools for assessing comprehension and critical-thinking skills and strategies.

 # Portfolio Opportunities

The portfolio icon indicates portfolio opportunities throughout the Paperback Plus Teacher's Resource.

Setting the Stage

BOOK SUMMARY

An ant, lying happily in the shade in the cow's backyard, invites one animal after another to climb in the hammock. Larger and larger animals join in: a frog, a chick, a hen, a duck, a cat, a dog, a lamb, and the cow. Then a huge elephant comes along. What will happen if *she* accepts the ant's invitation?

The elephant solves the problem and averts disaster by lifting the hammock—animals and all—onto her back.

INTRODUCING THE THEME

Focus Theme:
Sharing Time

Other Themes:
Say It Again!
Problem Solving
Weather
Summertime
Animal Life

Read the directions for "Sardines" on page 28, and invite children to play the game. Then use it to begin a discussion on sharing. At what point was the game most difficult to play? When was it the most fun? Would it be more fun with more players?

Encourage children to talk about their own experiences with sharing. Ask them to describe some times when sharing is fun. Are there times when it is hard to share?

BUILDING BACKGROUND

Spelling

For your spelling lists, you may want to use words from the Developing Vocabulary sections, other words from the book, or words from children's writing.

Share the magazine article "It's So-o-o Hot!" on pages 26–27. Discuss the ways those desert animals beat the heat. Then invite children to talk about how *they* like to spend hot afternoons. Ask what they do to cool off or to relax.

At the center of a sheet of chart paper, write *Ways to Keep Cool*. Invite volunteers to draw or write their ideas around it. If no one suggests *sit in the shade* as one of the entries, add it yourself.

Share the book with children, discussing the title, the table of contents, the author and illustrator biographies, and the dedication. You might do the following:

- Ask children what animals they see on the cover, what season of the year it is, and how the picture makes them feel. Invite them to tell what the ant might be thinking as it sees the cow relaxing in the hammock.

- After sharing the information about the author and the illustrator, ask what might happen if the animals in the story take a *siesta.*

- In their journals, children can record their thoughts, questions, jokes, funny stories, and drawings about experiences they have had with sharing. After reading, they can add their feelings about the ways the story characters share.

Bulletin Board Idea

Across a large bulletin board, make a hammock from colorful paper or cloth. Add the title "Relax with a Good Book." Children can make posters advertising their favorite books and display them in the hammock.

C H O I C E S   F O R   R E A D I N G

Exploring the Whole Book

Invite children to think about why families, friends, and classmates share things with each other. Use the questions below to help children set purposes before reading the book or to prompt discussion after reading.

Exploring the Book in Segments

The following are suggested breaks for exploring *In the Cow's Backyard.*

Segment 1: Come Join Us, *pages 2–9*

Segment 2: Larger and Larger Animals Climb In, *pages 10–17*

Segment 3: Potential Trouble When an Elephant Arrives, *pages 18–23*

Discussion Questions

1. Where does the story take place? Who are the characters? What is their problem, and how do they solve it? *(Story Structure and Summarizing)*

2. Why does the ant invite all the animals into the hammock? *(Inferences: Drawing Conclusions)*

3. Why do you think the animals feel so happy lying in the hammock? *(Inferences: Drawing Conclusions)*

4. Do you think the ant's idea to share the hammock is a good one or not? Why? *(Evaluating)*

5. What would happen if the elephant climbed into the hammock? *(Cause and Effect)*

Segment 1 Summary:
pages 2–9

- An ant lies happily in a shaded hammock as the cow gathers apples in her basket.

- One by one, a frog, a chick, and a hen come by and accept the ant's invitation to climb into the hammock.

- Everyone is happy. As the text assures us in each new scene, "it feels so nice to be in the shade!"

Assessment

- As children make predictions or answer discussion questions, note whether their answers are compatible with what they know about the story so far.

- Have children compare the story with other animal stories they have read.

- Note how children choose and complete the activities on page 7.

- Children can do Activity Master 1: All Together *(Language Patterns)* on page 13.

Developing Vocabulary

Ask children if they know what a hammock is. Sketch a simple hammock on the board or talk about the one on the cover of the book. Invite any children who have sat in a hammock to tell what supported it, how they climbed in, how many people could fit in it at one time, and whether it could swing or tip over.

Reading Strategies

Predict/Infer Take a picture walk through page 7, and then ask children to predict what might happen. As necessary, prompt them by asking what the animals will do and what might happen to the hammock. Record their predictions on chart paper so that children can check them later.

 Invite children to use their journals to record a question they expect to answer as they read the story.

Discussion Questions

1. Why do the animals think "it feels so nice to be in the shade"? *(Cause and Effect)*

2. What does the ant say each time a new friend appears? What other parts of the story are the same in each scene? *(Language Patterns)*

3. What do you think the ant is like? Would you say the ant is smart or silly? Friendly or mean? Give reasons for your answers. *(Inferences: Drawing Conclusions)*

4. Is this story real or make-believe? How do you know? *(Fantasy and Realism)*

ACTIVITIES

Choose one or more of these activities
to do by yourself or with a friend.

Language Arts: Keeping Cool

Look at the cow's backyard. What else could the ant do there to cool off? Make a list for the ant. Then choose one thing to draw and write about.

Drama: A Chat in the Hammock

What might the ant and the frog say to each other in the hammock? And what would they talk about with the chick and the hen?

Choose three partners. Act out what the animals would say and do.

Art: Last Summer

What do **you** do when the weather is hot? Draw a picture of something you did last summer. On the back, write to a friend and tell why it was a good way to cool off.

Language Arts: A Party Invitation

Write an invitation from the ant to its friends. Invite them to a hammock party. Tell when to come, where, and what kind of party it is. Tell what you will do for fun. Don't forget to sign the ant's name!

Segment 2 Summary:
pages 10–17

- Larger and larger creatures appear. Each is quickly issued an invitation by the friendly ant, who believes that there is always room for one more friend.

- Each new creature—a duck, a cat, a dog, a lamb—hops into the hammock.

Developing Vocabulary

Point out that authors often use sound words in stories to show when the animals speak. Begin a list of animals from the story so far and have children tell what they say. You might list several sounds for some animals.

ant	frog	chick	hen
no sound words	croak croak ribbit coquí coquí	cheep cheep peep peep pío pío	

Have children continue the chart by listing other animals and sound words. Suggest that partners take turns making the sounds and guessing the corresponding animals. Children can add to the list as they read more of the story.

Reading Strategies

Self-Question If children have not used their journals to record a question they expect to answer as they read the story, suggest that they do so now. If necessary, use these questions as prompts: What do you think the ant will say if new friends come by? What might happen to the hammock if more animals climb in? What might happen to make the story funny?

Monitor Remind children that readers can do several things if a selection does not seem to make sense: reread the text, look ahead to see what happens next, and/or look at the illustrations for help. Suggest that children use these ideas if they have trouble reading the next section.

Assessment

- Observe how children summarize the story. Note whether they include the important elements: characters, setting, problem. Ask them to propose a solution.

- Invite individuals to read aloud a favorite part. Listen for fluency as they read.

- Note how children choose and complete the activities on page 9.

- Children can do Activity Master 2: Which Came Next? *(Sequence)* on page 14.

Discussion Questions

1. Whom is the story about? What happens at the beginning? Is a problem starting to develop? Can you use these important parts of the story to summarize what has happened so far? *(Story Structure and Summarizing)*

2. What animals are in the story so far? Can you find a clue to help you remember the order in which they appear? *(Sequence)*

3. How do you think the animals feel as the hammock fills up? Do they look happy or worried? How would you feel? *(Noting Details; Inferences: Drawing Conclusions)*

4. Where do you think the cow is in this part of the story? What do you think she is doing? *(Inferences: Drawing Conclusions)*

5. What would you do if you were in the hammock with the animals? *(Personal Response)*

ACTIVITIES

Choose one or more of these activities
to do by yourself or with a friend.

A Memory Game

Make a circle with some friends. Say, "I went on a picnic and I took a blanket." The next player says what you said and adds one more thing.

Go around the circle. Each player repeats what was said and then adds one new thing. How long can you keep going?

Math: How Many Will Fit?

Draw a big hammock. Get blocks to use as counters. You will need two sizes.

About how many big counters will fit in the hammock? Write down a number. Use the counters to check. Now try it with the small counters.

Language Arts: Sharing Time

What can the animals in the hammock do for fun? Can they play games? Sing songs? Tell stories? Make a list. Choose one thing, and write about the animals having fun.

Science: Animal Report

Choose your favorite animal from the story. Use library books to find out more about it. Share what you learned. Tell the class where the animal lives, what it eats, and how large or small it is.

Segment 3 Summary:
pages 18–23

- Everyone is happily lying in the hammock in the shade.

- Suddenly an elephant appears. The animals wonder what the ant will say *this* time and what will happen if the elephant is invited to join them.

- Fortunately, the ingenious elephant lifts the hammock full of animals onto her back. With goodwill, there's always room for everyone to share in the fun.

Developing Vocabulary

Write *backyard* on the board or on chart paper. Ask a volunteer to divide the word and find the two shorter words within it.

Challenge children to write meanings for the two words. Then ask whether those definitions can help them define *backyard.* Have the group agree on a definition.

As children read the remainder of the story, ask if they can find the other compound word that the author uses. *(goodwill)*

Reading Strategies

Self-Question   After children read the story, have them refer to the questions they wrote in their journals. Were their questions answered? Did the story end the way they thought it would?

Evaluate   Ask children if they think any parts of the story are funny and why. Was the ending a surprise? How do they feel about the elephant's solution?

 You may want to invite children to play "Sardines" (page 28) again and lead them to conclude that a small space can contain only so many players.

Discussion Questions

1. What was the problem in the last part of the story? What was the solution? *(Story Structure and Summarizing)*

2. What do you think might have happened if the elephant had climbed into the hammock? *(Inferences: Making Predictions)*

3. What do you think the word *goodwill* means? What clues in the verse and in the animals' expressions on pages 22–23 can help you figure it out? *(Noting Details)*

4. What do you think happened during the animals' elephant ride? Where do you suppose they went? *(Inferences: Making Predictions)*

Assessment

- As children summarize and evaluate the story, note whether they identify the author's use of humor and surprise.

- Ask volunteers to tell how they would have ended the story.

- Note how children choose and complete the activities on page 11.

- Children can do Activity Master 3: Share-the-Pool Party *(Problem Solving)* on page 15.

WRAP-UP ACTIVITIES

After reading the book, choose one or more of these activities to do by yourself or with a friend.

Art: A Cartoon Strip

The little ant and the big elephant are friends. Think about what they could do together. Then make a funny cartoon strip to show one of their adventures. You may need 4 or 5 pictures. Share your strip with the class.

Language Arts: Interviews

Make a list of people you know. Ask each of them these questions:

- Can you remember a time when it was important to share?

- What happened?

Tell your classmates what you learned about sharing.

Art: My Favorite Animal

What is your favorite animal? Would it fit in the hammock? Draw a picture of the animal and write about how it could use a hammock.

Drama: Play Time

Make this story into a play. Get together with some friends. Choose what character you will be. Make up words to say. You might want to make up a new ending for your play.

PAPERBACK PLUS ACTIVITIES

Choose one or more of these activities
to do by yourself or with a friend.

**So Many Kinds of
Animals** (pages 24–25)
Language Arts

A Matching Game

Read the poem about the
animals. Look closely at the
picture. Can you find each
kind of animal the poet talks
about?

It's So-o-o Hot!
(pages 26–27)
Science

Desert Life

Find out more about plants
and animals that live in the
desert. What helps them live
in the hot, dry desert? Look in
library books.

It's So-o-o Hot!
(pages 26–27)
Science

More About the Sun

Find out information about
the sun. Tell how big it is, how
hot it is, and where it is. Draw
a picture of the sun to share as
you tell about it.

Sardines
(page 28)
Math

Guess How Many

Fill a jar with marbles or
pebbles. Count them as you
put them in. Hold a contest.
See who comes closest to
guessing the right number!

All Together

Name _____

Finish the sentences and cut them out. Paste them on other paper. Add pictures and make a book.

_____

A _____ goes by.

"Come join us," says the _____. ①

A _____ goes by.

② "Come join us," says the _____.

A _____ goes by.

"Come join us," says the _____. ③

"We can all sit together if we

_____

④ _____ "

Which Came Next?

Name _____

In the Cow's Backyard

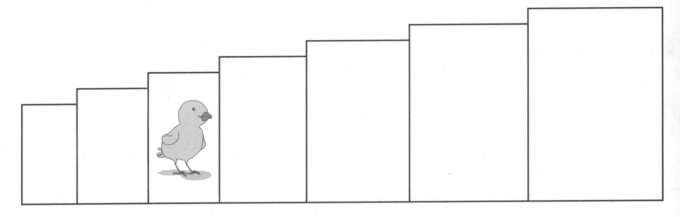

✂ Color and cut out the pictures below.
Paste them in order and retell the story.
Which clues help you remember the order?

Share-the-Pool Party

Name

ant	chick	duck	dog	elephant
frog	hen	cat	lamb	cow

How could all the animals play in one pool?
Share ideas with a friend.

✂ Cut out the pool. Paste it on art paper.
Now draw your best idea and write about it.

Reflecting/Self-Assessment

Make copies of the diagram below, and distribute them to children. Have them reflect on their experiences with reading the book and doing the activities.

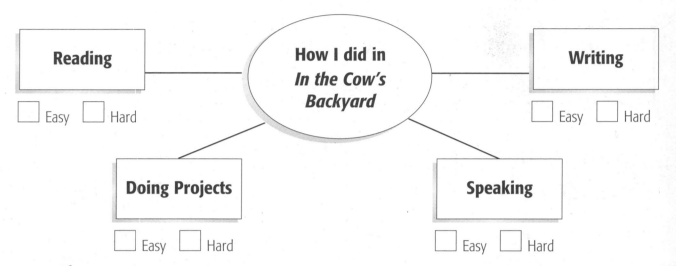

Reading	How I did in *In the Cow's Backyard*	Writing
☐ Easy ☐ Hard		☐ Easy ☐ Hard
Doing Projects		Speaking
☐ Easy ☐ Hard		☐ Easy ☐ Hard

INFORMAL ASSESSMENT CHECKLIST

Invite children to answer the following questions during conference time, or observe their performance levels in using the skills listed below.

Skill	Question/Activity	Beginning	Developing	Proficient
Monitor	Have children tell what they do when the text doesn't seem to make sense. (reread, read ahead, look at the pictures)			
Story Structure and Summarizing	Ask children to identify the characters' problem and solution. What would *they* have done? Have them write a new ending.			
Sequence	Make cards with the animals' names for children to put in the order they appear in the story. How would the story differ if the elephant got in the hammock first?			
Cause and Effect	This group of animal friends might want to play together again. What other problems might be caused by the size of the group?			